2/98

WILKINSON PUBLIC LIBRARY
1 23 0000307144

394 MAR
M   By er
P W

P9-CKB-847

POWWOW

POW WOW

Images along the Red Road

Photographs by Ben Marra

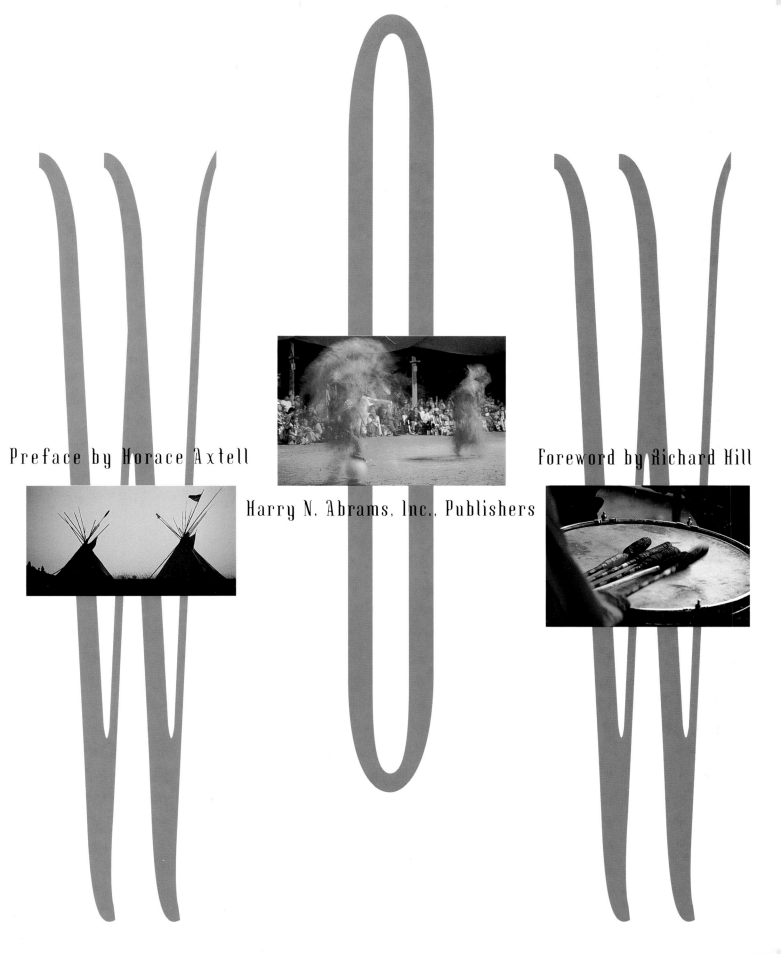

Preface by Horace Axtell

Foreword by Richard Hill

Harry N. Abrams, Inc., Publishers

CONT

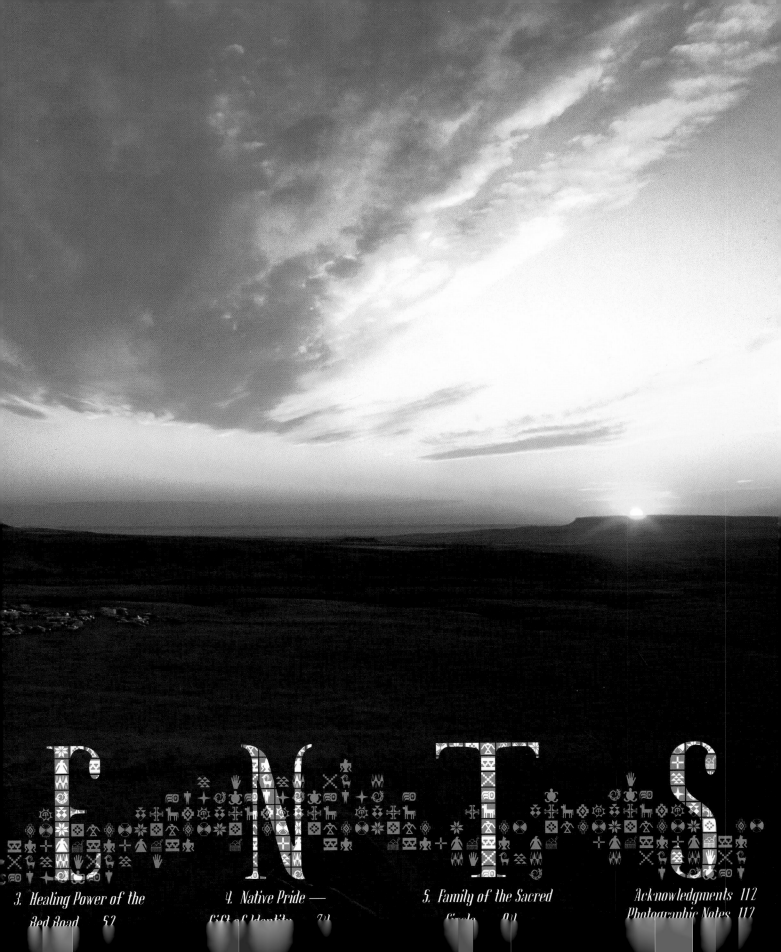

E·N·T·S

The Light in the Forest

by Richard W. Hill, Sr. (Tuscarora) Native American Studies, State University of New York at Buffalo

I used to say that the only good Indian, in modern America's mind, was a dancing Indian. Tourists, scholars, artists, and fairgoers all seemed to like Indians best when we were dressed to the hilt in feathers, beads, and war paint. When we danced, we were safe to consume. Unless we conformed to the stereotypes, most Americans did not want to hear from us. In this way of thinking, the powwow became a sort of Indian minstrel show in my mind, where Indians fiercely competed for prize money—to the delight of the non-Indian audience. I almost came to resent the powwow as the ultimate insult to our real dancing cultures.

But the power of the drum is just too much for me to resist, as it is with most Indians. No matter how far away I am when the drum starts its call and the singers crank up a good song, the powwow becomes an irresistible magnet, pulling me and hundreds of other people to it. The dance circle draws us in. The powwow has now spread coast to coast, and while some see it as a pan-Indian fabrication, I now see that it serves as a vital catalyst for cultural renewal. What makes this so? Certainly, the idea that Indians have been gathering to dance for longer than there has been a thing called the United States, makes the tradition of dance a powerful metaphor for expressing ancient beliefs that transcend modern realities. But this is not just about reliving the past. Each generation of Indians has to learn the songs for themselves, learn the traditions of their dances, learn how to make their own dance outfits, and, of course, learn how to dance in their own way. No matter how we dance, how we dress, or how we live, for the few moments of the song we stand together as a people, united by tradition and connected in the certain belief that dance is essential to the expression of ourselves. Be it a time-honored song or a new creation by the hottest drum, the act of dancing makes the powwow come alive. Powwow is not a spectator sport, despite the crowds that gather to watch Indian dancers. Powwow is for everyone, young and old, men and women, East and West, to share our sense of ourselves.

We have all heard that the drum is the heartbeat of the earth, that dancers move their feet in harmony with that heartbeat. We have all heard of the meaning of the dances, the symbolism of the clothing, and the sacredness of the feathers. But the real meaning of the dance cannot be explained. Magic happens when individuals take the time to make the beadwork and bustles, learn the songs and steps, and proudly step forward to express themselves through these dances. It is that magic that keeps me coming to the powwow, like sunlight that shines into dark woods as one pushes through to a clearing. The light makes the woods come alive. The quality of that light can only be enjoyed by being there. The powwow has become our light in a very dark world.

These photographs are a testimony to those individuals who make the powwow magic. They are the human element behind the traditions, the real people who keep it all going. They may be construction workers, computer operators, students, or blackjack dealers during the week. On weekends, however, the ageless drum calls again, not to help them relive their cultural past but to celebrate their real existence in the world. It is the dancers' faces in these photographs that speak to me the loudest, despite their very quiet demeanor. They tell me of themselves, determined and honor-bound to keep the dancing tradition alive. It is more than pride that I see. It is a faith in what their ancestors have given them, and it is also a faith that somehow the Creator will see them as they dance, not for the prize money but for the sake of the dance itself. For the powwow is a communal expression of belief that is shared by hundreds of individuals who gather from across the country to celebrate their uniqueness as the native people of this land. I am very grateful for that, and hope that you think of these thoughts as you look into the faces of these people.

This book is dedicated to "The Blacksmith."

Editor: Robert Morton
Designer: Robert McKee

*Library of Congress Cataloging-
in-Publication Data
Marra, Ben.
POWWOW / photographs by Ben
Marra; Preface by Horace Axtell;
foreword by Richard Hill.*
    p.   cm.
*ISBN 0–8109–2680–6 (pbk.)
1. Powwows. 2. Indians of
North America—Rites
and ceremonies.
3. Powwows—Pictorial works.
4. Indians of North America—
Rites and ceremonies—
Pictorial works. I. Title.
E98.P86M37 1996
394—dc20   96–6093*

*Copyright ©1996 Ben Marra
Published in 1996 by Harry N.
Abrams, Incorporated, New York
A Times Mirror Company
All rights reserved. No part of
the contents of this book may be
reproduced without the written
permission of the publisher
Printed and bound in Hong Kong*

*Right: Joseph L. Foltz, Yakama
Front cover: U-Lath-Quin-Sit
    Washington, Lummi
Back cover: Tasha June Cabanag,
    Turtle Mountain Chippewa /
    Yakama*

On the Red Road

Horace Axtell, Leader of the Seven Drum Religion, Nez Perce Reservation

I chose to become a traditional dancer because I strongly believe in our Indian way of life in every way. Being a veteran of World War II, I like to feel the strength of all warriors from the past and hear and dance to the old songs. Dancing and dressing in our finest regalia is one part of our way of life that includes participation by all ages: no one feels old when we dance. We have fun, and we also show respect to all the animals, birds, and earth materials we use to make our regalia and drums. The power of the spirits makes our songs; the spirits empower our singer-drummers to make our music. We gather many places all year to see old friends and make new friends.

We try to follow the footsteps of our elders, who cleared the way for us with their clean minds, hearts, and bodies. They walked in clean land, drank clean water, breathed clean air, and ate clean food provided by Mother Earth. This is the Red Road.

Most of these things we no longer have, but we still try to maintain what is left by building on the great spiritual foundation our ancestors and elders laid down. They prayed for our welfare, but their foresight could not cover such problems of today as drugs and alcohol. So, in order to keep the Red Road clean and good, as was intended by our ancestors, and also by elders we have known, we must be strong followers of our Indian ways. We must help all concerned people in the war against drug and alcohol problems, which threaten to destroy our young today.

This is why all our powwows are kept free of drugs and alcohol. We can have good, clean fun and enjoy the Red Road with dignity as it was intended.

Introduction

Until eight years ago, I had never been to a powwow, nor did I know what a powwow was. I had only seen Native Americans dancing once before. I was bike riding in Discovery Park, a pristine wooded area just outside Seattle, and stopped to rest at the Daybreak Star Art and Cultural Center. There, I watched a performance by a small group of dancers. I was delighted with the gorgeous display of colorful outfits and the rhythmical singing and drumming. Rested, and warmed by what I had seen, I continued on my ride.

Years later, after returning from a month photographing in Nepal, I was invited by a Seattle printing company to think of an idea and supply a photograph to promote their latest printing techniques. The theme was "Celebrate Washington." I rejected apples, salmon, and the timber industry, and suggested instead that I photograph descendants of the first people to call Washington home—the North American Indians. Little did I know that this would become a turning point in my career.

I proposed the idea to the printing company on a Thursday. They liked it very well, but asked me to have the transparencies for them on the following Monday. After a few hurried phone calls, I was able to reach one of the men I had watched dance years before at the park. He graciously invited me to photograph at a powwow scheduled that very weekend at a local school, where he was the principal.

My wife, Linda, and I arrived at the school and found ourselves in an unusual photographic situation. I wanted to make portraits of the dancers, so I needed an area for my backdrop and lighting equipment. But the only place I could set up my makeshift studio was in a hallway, under a low ceiling and among the kids' lockers. As we got things ready, we could hear the sounds of drumming, singing, and dancing in the gymnasium down the hall and around a corner. We were tantalized.

While I stayed with my cameras in my "studio," Linda took a deep breath and crept into the crowded gym. It was filled with the sounds of thundering drums and high-pitched singing voices. Painfully aware that she was the only non-Indian in the room, Linda cautiously approached some of the dancers and invited them to be photographed.

Her sincerity and forthright charm worked. One by one, she led them to me. That evening, we photographed eleven people and began our new lives as photographers of powwow dancers. One of the men we photographed that first night appears in this book (see page 80). His name is George Kicking Woman, and he is one of the primary traditional spiritual leaders of the Blackfeet Nation. He and his wife, Molly, had driven 622 miles to the Seattle powwow from their home in Browning, Montana. This was our first experience of a powwow and we were overwhelmed and fascinated by the people we were meeting.

When we looked at the results of that night's work, we discovered that I had recorded more than just colorful images or fabulous outfits. We felt that I had recorded a sense of the people's spirituality, dignity, and proud identity. The images had a regal quality; we sensed that we had been allowed a glimpse of history and heritage—and that we had been privileged to make art in response to it.

Since 1988, Linda and I have been to dozens and dozens of powwows where we have photographed hundreds of dancers. Powwows became a breath of fresh air in our city-bound lives. We'd load up the old Jeep Grand Wagoneer, leave the traffic and madness behind, and take off for the plains of Montana, complete with our bumper-sticker proclaiming, "Custer wore arrow shirts." Recently, we have been invited to attend private ceremonies, which is a great honor for us. We recognize, however, that this is not our culture and we have not become members of the "wanna-be tribe." We haven't done a "sweat," we have no plans for a "piercing," and we don't "smudge" our studio for protection. Our respect for native culture, however, is profound and sincere.

At the powwows, we receive permission to set up the photography equipment in an area slightly away from the dancing circle. We try to be nearby, because we do not have much time with our subjects; they are there to dance and socialize with their extended families and friends. Usually I have less than ten minutes with each person. Linda says it is my gift to be able to connect instantly with them, to gain their acceptance and trust and then shoot—fast. Linda records each subject's personal and tribal information. Afterward, we send everyone a series of duplicate slides for their own use. We do not place the images in stock photo libraries, and no photograph is ever used by us for any purpose without the expressed permission of the individual. We have selected four photographs for a limited edition print series, called The Powwow Editions. Proceeds from the sale of these images are shared with the subjects.

Our years on the powwow trail have taught us a lot about these people and their culture. We now understand that the powwows are more than just social occasions. The people have chosen a path of commitment, a way of life. They say that they dance to follow the Red Road, which means they have chosen to live free of alcohol and drugs. Many Native Americans have experienced firsthand or close-up the devastations of alcohol and drug abuse. They believe deeply that substance abuse short-circuits a natural connection to Spirit and the ancient teachings of Mother Earth's healing properties. By making the commitment to follow the Red Road and dance on the powwow trail, their connection with the Creator can become strong again. Dancing enables them to heal their wounds and live with honor and pride in being Indian. And so alcohol and drugs are prohibited at powwows. The Red Road is a healing path for Indian identity—in both body and spirit—a path to the Creator.

Photography has proven to be a fortunate career for me, and my work photographing on the powwow trail has enlivened my own spirit and filled many long, happy weekends. In 1973, after graduating from Brooks Institute of Photography, I decided to establish my studio and focus on corporate assignments. My regular commercial work continues during the week in a studio in a renovated old hotel building in Seattle's Pioneer Square. Coincidentally, one hundred years ago, Edward Curtis, another white man who loved to photograph Indians, had his photography studio a few blocks from here. I feel a great connection with him, and with other photographers who have accepted Indian hospitality and been allowed to photograph these handsome, proud people.

We have particularly loved photographing the tribal children. They are being raised to honor their elders, and they are being taught, by example, the value of storytelling in keeping alive the legends and traditions of their people. Many of the kids tell us, when they see us at a subsequent powwow, that they have displayed my photographs in their homes, or given them as gifts to favorite relatives, especially grandparents. We are proud to contribute these images to their heritage. As a result of being allowed to photograph the Red Road, we have been able to give something back to our subjects.

Powwows used to be strictly social events, but after about the 1920s they also became the sites of contest dancing. Now, dancers compete for prize money in categories based on age, dancing style, and regalia. The regalia of dancers, which they sometimes call "outfits," provide the explosion of color captured by my lens. The outfits, however, are much more than beaded and feathered costumes. They are expressions of a dancer's personal and tribal history, although many dancers adopt regalia styles and accessories of other tribes. Thus, dancers also learn much about the traditions of others.

As much as I am excited by the outfits of the dancers, more importantly I am captivated by their faces, and by the enormous pride and dignity they reveal to my camera. When we began to assemble images for this book we realized that we wanted to include more than just the pictures, so Linda took on the job of collecting and helping to record the subjects' own words to accompany their photographs. She asked them simply to write their feelings about why they dance and what it means to them. We have tried to create here for our readers—and for our subjects as well—a close approximation of our own very moving experiences on the powwow trail.

Ben Marra

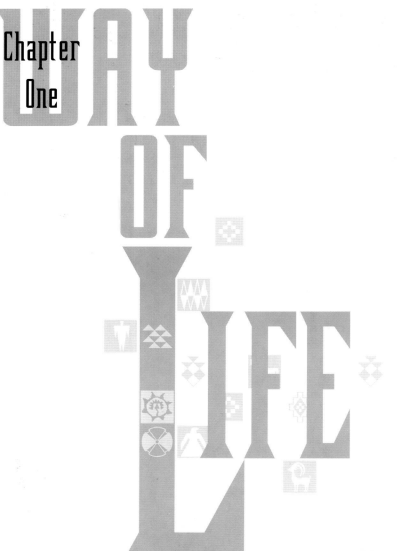

Chapter One

WAY OF LIFE

Alex Williams, Jr. ◆ Nez Perce

Tradition is a thing of great importance. I have
been taught to balance education and tradition.
We must not let traditions die away, because if
they die, then we as a people will cease to exist.
As long as I am alive, that will never happen. I
have been taught much that is good by many
people. It is always said that you must learn of
your people, but how is that possible without
someone to teach. Our ancestors suffered so
that we may live. What they taught, we should
carry on. The things we say or do will reflect on
us. So, if we do what is right, we will all be proud.

Chief William DePoe
Siletz/Cheyenne

Returning home from the Navy as a decorated World War II veteran (my ship was sunk at Okinawa), I looked back to my Indian roots and realized how rapidly the cultures were being lost and how little understanding there was of my people. I was moved to combine my love of music with my culture to write original Indian compositions and to tell legends to be passed on. When I dance I wear traditional Plains Indian clothing, and an eagle feather headdress, which represents my years of service and accomplishments. The arrows on my face are marks given to me as a child by the medicine man; they indicate protection. I carry dancing sticks with white feathers that the children can touch.

Dan Nanamkin
Nez Perce/Okanogan

For me, dancing is a way of life. Since I have joined the circle, there is not a day that goes by that I don't sing or dance. Whether I am alone, at work, home, or traveling to the next powwow, I think of the old days, how our ancestors enjoyed themselves dancing, what it must have meant to them, and the stories that they told. I think of my grandfathers, the warriors who fought in battle and danced in victory. These things are in my heart as I dance in the circle. When I pound the ground, I feel a closeness and a relationship between myself and all my relations on the dance floor and those who have passed on.

I dance for our children who need role models in this modern society. I try hard to follow, learn and abide by our ways, so that I, too, may pass this on to our next generation. I dance for those of us who are disabled. I dance hard and pound the floor for them. If they could, you bet they would be dancing hard too. I will dance for them so they may feel the vibration of the drum. I dance for our elderly, people who have passed the knowledge of traditions and language to our generation. They are the ones who have seen us grow. In respect, I want them to feel proud and I want them to see that I care for them. I want them to know that in my heart I will try to carry on this tradition that they have passed on to us. I want to help them in prayers and thoughts as I dance around this circle. May they be happy and live well.

Mary, Jennifer, Joyce Everybodytalksabout

Colville/Blackfeet

Our cultural heritage is shared between the Colville and Blackfeet tribes; Plateau and Plains Indians. We come from a large, proud family often seen at powwows. We love to dress in our finest regalia and dance as often as possible.

(The girls are wearing traditional dresses for dancing. Buckskin dresses are usually heavily beaded across the yoke and have long fringes on the sleeves and along the bottom.)

(Left) James "Hoody" Walsey, Pas-ta-xit

Warm Springs/ Wailaki/Yakama/ Shoshone-Bannock

(Right) Keno Colby White

Yakama/Dineh

James: I started dancing when I was about one year old, and at five I began singing at powwows too. With the help of my uncle and my grandpa, I became the lead singer for the Eagle Spirit Singers from the Yakama Valley. My Indian name, Pas-ta-xit, was passed down from my great-grandfather who was a spiritual leader. Then, it was given to my grandfather, who gave the name to me. We now share Pas-ta-xit together. The outfit I'm wearing was made by my father, mother, and oldest sister.

Hollyanna Decoteau Pinkham-Spino

Yakama/Nez Perce

It's a way of life to sing, dance and drum
To the heart beat, the heart beat of the people,
The heart beat of mother earth.
There is no life without a heart beat.
Dance for life.

Gary E. Greene ◆ Nez Perce

Dancing is my strength, it provides me with a way of building and restoring pride of my culture. It's an instrument that enables me to share and teach others what little I know. It allows me to honor the traditions of our elders who hold it in a sacred way. It helps me to dance with the older ones and to share a smile, a handshake, and maybe a story. It's more than dancing—it's a way of life.

Jackie Carson ◆ Flathead/Nez Perce

I am the great-granddaughter of Sum-Keen, a nephew of Young Chief Joseph. As a child, I had always been involved in the powwows. In high school, as a member of the Indian Club, I went to neighboring schools to exhibit our regalia and explain Native American culture. I have been active in competition dancing and appear in parades with full horse regalia. I have always done my own beadwork, and am sometimes called upon to do outfits for others. I welcome the opportunity to explain the Indian culture to non-Indians, so they will have a better understanding.

Lawrence V. Augustine
(1944–1993) ◆ Micmac

In powwow life, wherever you set up your tepee, you feel home and welcome. It is a pleasure to see how young people care for the elders and how elders share their memories. As an Army man, being forced to change places every three years, this kind of life was a wonderful discovery.

Because of our regalia, many members of other East Coast tribes, drawn to the drums, recognized us: we were glad to see each other. We also met many Vietnam veterans following the drum. When you are together out on the dancing arena, everybody knows you have come a long way. You show that you are determined not to fall back into dejection or alcoholism— and the drum keeps you going.

(Written by his wife, Marina H. Augustine.)

Leon Rattler ◆ Blackfeet

Dancing is a way of life, a gift that was given to me by my family. The Feather Belt Dance is a longtime tradition of the Blackfeet Nation. I proudly carry the belt in today's Indian dances. I remember getting ready to dance in the tepee of my grandmother, Mary Little Bull. The floor was covered with buffalo robes; I remember the color of the painted tepee liners, the parfleche bags and backrest. It gave me a feeling of being part of a great history; a history that gives me great pride as I dance in the footsteps of my elders of the Blackfeet Nation.

Leroy L. Seth ◆ Nez Perce

I started dancing when I was three years old. My grandfather used a hand drum, and he and my grandmother would sing. My cousins and I got our beginning this way.

Powwows start with the drum and Grand Entry; next comes the flag song; then prayer by a respected elder. Next follows a song to bring in the eagle feathers, flags, or colors. Recognition is made about the royalty, then a song is sung to open the powwow officially.

When I dance, whether I'm dancing the fancy, traditional, or grass-dance, I turn into another person, or spirit: I am in another world. Some songs make me feel lighter and able to get the natural high. I feel like many things: birds, animals, the wind, grass, and the difference between light and darkness. When I dance it brings me closer to the spirits of my loved ones and makes me feel good. I want to dance as long as my legs can do it.

Rikki Wahchumwah ◆ [Left]
and Donovan Howtopat ◆ [Right]

Mid-Columbia River tribes

At right, a bustle view of Rikki Wahchumwah

Michael Roberts (Dancing Eagle Feathers) ◆ Choctaw/Chickasaw

When I am dancing I feel the spirits of past generations. I feel if I dance hard enough, I can somehow help those that are in need. To dance is to feel free. I feel individuality in my style of dance. I give respect to my elders. I bring respect to myself, my family, and all my rela- tions. All of my life the arena has been part of me. I honor my family and friends for their help and understanding. I feel it is our respon- sibility to pass on the teachings of our elders to our children. Let our children not forget the way of our past and our people.

Stephen Small Salmon

Pend d'Oreille Flathead

When I was very little I remember my grandpa holding my hand and walking me to the dancing arbor in Arlee, Montana. I had a little black outfit with fringes. I could hear the drums as we walked. I remember how anxious I was to dance. I still feel the same way whenever I hear the drums. The drums are sacred, the ground we dance on is sacred. We dance in a circle, to us the circle is sacred.

Fifteen years ago, I remembered my grandpa's black leather outfit and scavenger with brass beads and buttons. So I designed and made my own black leather and fringe outfit with brass and silver. I dreamed the design and took my uncle's colors: red, yellow, and orange. I still wear this outfit. I also have a blue beaded outfit my mother, Mary Small Salmon, made about thirty years ago. She beaded it in the old way, tying every second bead. It takes many, many hours to do it this way. I chose this particular powder blue because it represents the sky. The star symbol, vest, and apron is a typical Flathead design. We paint our faces in the Flathead way, to protect us from our enemies and the evil spirits.

Vivian Theresa Cochran (Kills in the Brush)

Gros Ventre (Atsina)

When I was very young living at the Fort Belknap Reservation in Hays, Montana, my mother's uncle lived with us. He and his wife used to talk to us about our people, traditions, stories, customs, language, dances, and songs. I recall the elders, all dressed up in their buckskins and the women with their pretty dresses and moccasins. There was so much feeling, grace, honor, and pride. That is why I dance: the powwow is vital and special to me. I carry one eagle feather, which is my messenger of love, honor, and respect. At the powwow each one listens to the drum; it's like your own heartbeat, guiding you in your dances. Long after the honor song has ended a powwow, you can still feel the friendship and hear the drumming and songs.

Dawn DePoe

Cheyenne/Chippewa/Seneca/Tututni

When I first started dancing I was alone. No one danced before me in my family. When I began, my Mom told me, "Winning doesn't matter, just get out there and show your stuff. Be proud. Your time will come." Such words helped me strive for excellence. I would count the days until the next powwow. Friends from the powwow trail became my second family. Warm smiles and handshakes greeted me at every powwow. Now, each weekend I may dance at a different circle, with new people, but I still feel at home.

The familiar beat of the drum always calls me back, back to dance and make friends. Dancing at powwows is not just a hobby or a pastime to me, dancing is a way of life. Dancing is being proud: proud of your traditions, your family, and especially of yourself.

Nellie Two Bulls, Zintka To win (Blue Bird Woman)

Oglala Sioux

When I was twelve years old I had a vision that held many gifts for my life's journey and also brought me my name. I dreamed of three women. The first, dressed in yellow, offered beautiful gifts of quillwork, and said that I would know how to do such work without instruction. The second, dressed in red, carried feather and beadwork that I could make with my small hands. The third, called "Blue Bird Woman" brought a drum full of songs. She said that among the many birds that fly south for the winter only the bluebird would stay. She told me that I would be a singer and speaker, and that I must never be selfish with my voice, that I would never run out of songs. "Blue Bird Woman" would have a voice to cheer people all over the world. My life has been filled with song and dance.

CHAPTER TWO ANCESTRAL

BLESSING

DAVID J. MILLS
BLOOD

I was brought up traditionally and taught to respect my elders and their ceremonies. They taught me the songs and the ways of our people: how to do beadwork, make drums and dancing outfits, and keep our own language. I left all this for a while when I was sent to a boarding school for ten years, but I never forgot our ways.

I've been dancing for about seventeen years, and I am a member of the Sun Dancers on the Blood Indian Reserve in Standoff, Alberta, Canada. My outfit is black and yellow, like that of a bumble bee. The reason is that my grandfather's name was Bumble Bee Crow Chief. So I use his name at times and wear his colors at every powwow. I carry my pipe and eagle-bone whistle. I love my grandfather very much, and this is a way I can show my love for him and my parents for the love and support and teaching they gave me.

EDITH JOHNSON/
WALSEY, SAU-PIN

WARM SPRINGS / WAILAKI / YAKAMA

I am an enrolled member of the Confederated Tribes of the Warm Springs Reservation of Oregon. Additionally, I have Wailaki and Yakama blood. I started dancing when I was around nine years old. My entire family dances at powwows, including my children.

My mom had this outfit I'm wearing made for me when I was about fifteen years old. After a while, it was stolen from me. I continued to search for it, hoping someday I would find it. Finally, after thirteen years, I saw

my dress being worn by a dancer at a powwow in Arlee, Montana. When I approached her, she said she had bought it at a pawn shop. It took another year to reclaim my dress, but today
I wear it with great pride.

AL BLACKBIRD
OMAHA

The designs and colors of my regalia all have a very special meaning to me. My Indian name simply means "star" and I am from the Thunder clan. I use the four-point star design. Each point represents one of the sacred four directions.

My grandfather, Theodore White, Sr., and my uncle, Rufus White, were an inspiration to me. I was able to learn from them about my culture and background. My grandfather passed away when I was very young. I can still remember dancing with him in the sacred circle. I would like to dedicate all my dancing to my grandfather.

JIM LABELLE, TA-SHUN-KA-DUZA-HAN (HIS HORSE FAST)

SISSETON SIOUX

I am a descendant of the last chief of the Sisseton Sioux, whose name was Gabriel Renville, Ti-Wakan (Holy Lodge). He was my great-great-grandfather. The pictograph on my vest shows peace between soldiers and the Sioux. My people fought for thirty years for our land. When I dance at a powwow it means a lot to me, and I want people to know I am Indian and proud. When I was a child, my grandparents would take me to dances in a wagon drawn by a team of horses. I would watch the dancers and say, "someday, I will be dancing like them." I am a grandfather now, and I encourage my grandchildren to dance.

HARVEY RUNNING CRANE WHITFORD, E-TUCK-SIS-TOI-YEE (MANY NIGHT BOY)

BLACKFEET

I was born on the Blackfeet Indian Reservation in Browning, Montana. My Indian name was given to me by my grandmother, Annie Short Robe. We call ourselves the children of the prairies because our ancestors once roamed the Great Northern Plains. When I was a boy, I remember helping my cousins put up my grandmother's tepee during our annual celebration in Browning. I used to watch the dancers late at night. The drums would put me to sleep as I lay in my grandmother's tepee looking up at the stars through the smoke hole of the lodge. Now I am a traditional dancer and have been given the right to carry the eagle bone whistle because I am a veteran. The sage and sweet grass is my medicine; the eagle is my guide; the Creator is my protector. My outfit was made by my family and beaded by my brother, Night Hawk Red Star, and his wife, Sandra. My dance is the traditional dance and I follow in the steps of my grandfathers to keep our culture alive.

KEVIN HAYWAHE (POWERFUL WALKING WOLF)

ASSINIBOINE

I belong to the Carry The Kettle Assiniboine Tribe and I have been dancing since early boyhood. As I dance, I will carry on. I would like to thank the Great Spirit, my family, chief and council, and pay special homage to my late grandfather, Albert Eashappie, who was a tribal healer. He gave me his blessings to be the champion traditional dancer I am today.

P.R. BARRIL
TLINGIT

My name is Crying Raven. I am from the Community House called Takdeintaan Hit. The family crest is the Humpback Whale under the Raven Tribe. My regalia was made by my grandmother, Shleinaan Klaa, and my aunts from the Eagle Tribe (KaagWaanTaan). Grandmother taught me everything about our culture: language, dancing, chants and our complicated society. In turn, I have a dance group, Ku-Tee-Ya (Totem), and I teach them everything I know so it won't be lost.

LOLITA HENRY
NEZ PERCE / COLVILLE

U–LATH–QUIN–SIT WASHINGTON

LUMMI

I was raised speaking my native tongue, and lost it at an early age when I was sent away to school. I was fortunate to have been raised by my beloved grandparents, learning the old ways, going to powwows to see the dancing and the stick games in which my grandfather excelled.

On weekends my family and I travel to powwows. As we drive up I feel like a small child again, all jittery with excitement as I hear and feel the drums surge through me like lightning.

I am a traditional dancer. My bustle is made from my first eagle, passed to me by my grandfather. My cuffs were beaded by him as well; my jewelry was given to me by my granny. When I dance, I don't think about competition or money, I pray to my Creator. Every step I take is a prayer. I think and remember my grandparents, I feel the sadness that my grandmother never got to see me dance, but I know that she watches me now from the spirit world.

When I dance, I dance from my soul.

ROSE ANN ABRAHAMSON

LEMHI SHOSHONE
"AQUI–TIKA"

My people were Sacajawea's people. We were raised with a deep respect for tradition, culture, and the joy of dancing. My role model was my father, Wilford George, who was a champion men's traditional dancer in the 1960s and 70s and taught me the purpose of dancing. He told me that as a dancer, we represent our people when we go out to dance. He said that the parts of the animals and birds we are wearing come alive again when we dance. We make the eagle fly again when we bring the fan up over the people. A woman blesses her people with her fan when she waves it over them as she dances within the sacred circle. So, I remember the teachings of my father, and wear the green beaded dress made by my loving mother, Camille, as I continue to dance with pride in the footsteps of my father and my Lemhi ancestors.

STERLIN WAHCHUMWAH
MID-COLUMBIA RIVER TRIBES / OKANAGAN

SHADOW WALKS TAILFEATHERS
BLACKFEET / CREE

My last name was earned by my great-great-grandfather of Browning, Montana. He was hunting as a young man and came upon a buffalo and wounded the animal. He chased it for many days. The buffalo ran up a rolling hill on the plains, and as it ran, a big golden eagle flew over. Later he came upon the buffalo lying before him with the eagle perched on top of it. He decided that he would take the eagle's life as well as the buffalo's. Our name comes from that moment.

My dancing comes from the Windyboy family of Rocky Boy, Montana. I was told that I began dancing at the time of my first walk. My grandparents taught me a spiritual awareness of the dancing—the feeling of the rhythm, like the rain dancing on mother earth, with no boundaries. The flexibility of the body is a great gift from the Creator. The sound of the drum makes your blood rush; your heart beats like the drum. The sweat runs across your face like a waterfall after the song is silent. Dance and song become one; your existence in the rhythm is like the wind rushing through the air.

TAMARA ARLENE JAMES, WASH-WII

YAKAMA/COLVILLE

The dress I'm wearing belongs to my grand-mother, who got it from my great-grand-mother, who traded for it from a member of the Crow tribe.

STEVEN REUBEN

NEZ PERCE

I like to dance for my people to the songs I remember my grandfather singing.

TASHA JUNE CABANAG

TURTLE MOUNTAIN CHIPPEWA/YAKAMA

I started dancing before I could walk. Mom says she had me in moccasins and a wing dress while I still was in my baby-board. I love to dance jingle, but I know I'll spend many years as a traditional dancer. My grandmother made my buckskin dress. It is moose-hide, which was given to her during a journey to Alberta, Canada. She spent many years gathering the beads for the dress. My grandmother has been unable to continue beading because her fingers become raw from the needles; also the beads are no longer made in the colors of my dress. The hair wraps I wear are of otter skins; eagle feathers hang from beaded rosettes and porcupine medallions. I carry a shawl, a beaded purse, and one other item that means so much to me—an eagle feather fan my Uncle Rainbow made for me.

WILLIAM MOORE, O'SKINA WAH

PRAIRIE BAND POTAWATOMI

I was taught to dance by an elder who would drum for me and encourage me to dance in several styles. I always felt good when I went to ceremonial dances or participated in other similar events. I will continue to dance to honor our heritage.

ELMER THOMAS ST. JOHN—BROWN
SISSETON—WAHPETON DAKOTA NATION

Dance means culture, heritage, religion, and family. Stories, history, and reverence are conveyed through music and dance. The drum represents the essence of life. At powwows or ceremonies the drum and singers bring the people together. It's the drum and the songs that make up the heart of dance. My family and I dance at powwows because it brings us together with family and friends. It's always a great feeling to be out there in the dance circle. I dance the traditional old style that was taught to me as a boy by my grandfathers, Elmer St. John and Tom Brown, Sr. They have both made the journey to the spirit world, but I know they are with me when I dance.

Chapter Three

Healing Power of the Red Road

Albert C. Thomas
Colville Confederated Tribes

Knowledge of my traditional cultural background has given me courage and motivation in my life. I have worked hard to become a traditional dancer, and have been attending powwows for many years. Prior to dancing, I was a drummer.

I feel I have earned respect from my family and community and have devoted myself toward helping the Native American community in Spokane and the surrounding reservations. I am currently working as Intern Director for the Native American Addictions Program. I feel a major concern that the pressures existing when I was growing up on a reservation are now more severe for the youth of today.

Rainbow Azure
Chippewa/Yakama
Bustle view at left.

Letitia Reddest
Jicarilla Apache/Cheyenne River Sioux

I believe that when the Great Spirit creates an individual, he or she is granted a special gift. My gift is my dancing ability. The colors in my dancing outfit are taken from the rainbow and the grass. These colors I wear symbolize the beauty of Mother Earth. The shawl I wear symbolizes the wings of a bird flying in the air.

Kenny Shane
Crow

Powwows have always made me happy, and the best
way I know to express happiness is through dancing. My
Dad once told me to dance for all the old people, for
those who are not as fortunate as you are, for all who
are sick or unhealthy: dance for life.

Bleu Jaye Kenoras
Yakama

Carolyn Running Crane Whitford, Tsa-Koeem Neema (Catches Last)

Coushatta/Blackfeet

The geometric pattern on my outfit is a traditional Blackfeet design. The four directions are depicted throughout the design in shape and color. Red, yellow, black and white stand for the people of Mother Earth. The shells represent the Coushatta nation, whose strength comes from the garfish, the sustainer of life. The blue is spiritual. It represents purification from the waters poured on the rocks in the sweat lodge. When I dance, my fringes brush away the bad spirits, so that when my eagle fan is raised high toward the sun, my prayers will reach the Creator for the good of all.

My name was given to me by my adopted father, Percy Bull Child of the Blackfeet Nation. He wrote The Sun Came Down, *a history of the Blackfeet as told to him by his grandmother, Catches Last.*

Burdick Two Leggins and Quentin Big Medicine ◆ Crow

At left is Burdick Two Leggins, crane stick bearer of the Black Lodge District Daytime Ceremonial War Dance Society of the Crow Tribe. Quentin Big Medicine carries the men's horse whip in the ceremony. He is Keeper of the Peace Pipe. To the Crow the powwow is of religious significance. The Crow derived the war dance from the vision of a young warrior left behind after a battle because of his injuries. He was healed when a crane came toward him carrying a sharp pointed stick trimmed with beadwork. The stick turned into a human being, who danced with other members of the animal kingdom and instructed the visionary young warrior to bring the crane-head stick back to the Crow people. It has been used in the Crow Daytime Ceremonial Dance for centuries. In the dance, the crane stick bearer prays for all by dancing to the four cardinal directions. The crane stick owner, the "feeder," sways his body three times in accompaniment to a song, and rises to dance at the fourth intonation of it. Toward the end, he swoops, and suddenly stops dancing as the drum ceases. He points his stick toward the north. As soon as the drumming and singing resumes, he dances as before, and when the drumming ceases again, he points his stick westward. Thus, he moves around in a circle, covering each quadrant.

Considered very sacred among the Crows, this ceremony is held only in the spring at the returning of the birds. During the Crow Daytime Ceremonial, gifts of all kinds are given to old and young of the tribe, as well as to visitors from other tribes. This represents the warrior's responsibility that everyone should be provided for.

Donald Rain
Stoney

My father had the greatest influence on me. He loved to dance and knew how to express his feelings while dancing. Proudly watching him made me realize that I could discover my own powwow trail, as he had. I sometimes feel a certain magic in the air when I travel to a powwow, and I know it will be special. I think of my father; like him, I love to dance. It gives me a sense of freedom in a world where there is too much confinement.

Marzha Lazelle Fritzler, Á-she-li-ih-chish
Crow/Laguna Pueblo

My identity as a member of the Ap-sáa-looke tribe was implanted by my great-grandmother's teachings, and her encouragement that we all participate in Crow tribal activities. Her husband was the son of the famous Crow scout at the battle of Little Big Horn, White Man Runs Him. She wanted each of us to have traditional Crow dress and she made sure each of us was given a Crow name. My dress is tanned buckskin and my leggings, belt, and moccasins are of traditional Crow design.

I was very fortunate to have known my great-grandmother during the first 14 years of my life. She was nearly one hundred years old when she passed on. I will always remember the first prayers that she taught me when I was little; this was at Crow Fair, with the beat of the drums in the background. I remember, when I was even younger, how she would lightly clap her hands, singing the Whistling Water Clan song in the Crow tongue, and how she would have all us young ones dancing. She gave me the name Á-she-li-ih-chish, a name that came to her in a dream she had about the strong medicine that the Sun Dance pole held.

Now my great-grandmother has joined Ak-baa-tat-día, but my grandmother, Minnie Ellen White Man Runs Him/Fritzler, has taken her place in the teachings. I thank Ak-baa-tat-día for the closeness within my family, for it is said that the poorest Crow is a Crow without a family. I hope that in this I will always remember where I came from and who I am in whatever I attempt.

Juanita Marcus Turley
Taos Pueblo

My Tiwa language and native teachings and ways have been the primary and major influences in my world. My father, Ben Marcus, provided the spark that encouraged me and my brothers and sisters to become enthusiastic about dancing and singing. From an early age, we participated in powwows, show dancing, and in our village dances and rituals. My mother, Manuelita, made sure that we had our outfits ready for these dances. Later in life, I traveled with my daughters and various family members to the Dakotas and other states where we took part in numerous celebrations and powwows. Powwows have given me the opportunity to travel, meet old friends, and make new friends. The dancing and singing offer a "natural high." No drugs or alcohol are needed or desired. I know that other native people share these feelings with me, and it is my hope that more of them will find joy on the powwow circuit as I have.

Greves Beaver
Stoney

John S. Ground III
Blackfeet

*In 1973 I received a head injury and I was left para-
lyzed on my right side. I underwent therapy in the
Army until my discharge in 1975. After my discharge,
I began working on my dancing regalia. I began dancing
and my culture and traditions really helped me overcome
my paralysis. For me, dancing has been a healing and
learning experience. I owe my knowledge of my culture
and traditions to my elders, ancestors, and the pursuit of
Indian pride.*

Elder Joe Roberts III, Tel-A-Sut and Snul-Thul-Ken II
Nooksack/Lummi

The regalia that I wear was made by me and my family. The eagle feathers that I wear are special to me because of their powers and strength. I would like to thank the elders who spent the time to share their teachings with me. It is my hope that one day I can pass my learning on to our younger generation.

Randy Vendiola (left)
Michael Vendiola (right)
Swinomish Tribe

We have pride in all the Native American cultures and we believe that the European American society is important as well. This is why we (and our older brother and sister) dance in the powwow and also are graduates at the university level. Education is our weapon of choice for today's battles. We are proud that, traditionally, Native Americans never had drugs or alcohol in their communities. This fact of our culture must be honored.

Monica Sue Russell, Mun-ho-wut (Spirit Woman)

Southern Cheyenne

When I dance I wear an eagle feather in my hair that had belonged to my grandfather, who was a chief for our people. His name was Harvey Russell, or Ishi-ivi, which means "Sun Chief." The bead-work that I wear was made by my mother, LeeAnna Russell. When I dance I feel proud to be a Native American representing my people in a good way. This means that I would never disrespect my people, the outfit that I wear, and the people I represent by engaging in activities such as drinking alcohol, using drugs, or being involved with gangs. It is impor-tant that I do my part in keeping my culture alive by dancing. Hopefully, I will set a good example for the younger generation, especially my son, Ricky. Practicing my heritage is not only important for me but also my family and my people. When I dance I feel happy knowing that my grand-mother was the one who influenced me. It's as if she is still in the crowd, smiling at me and waiting for me to take a break so that she can give me some advice. It is my hope that one day I will be a grandparent in the crowd, smiling at my grandchildren and giv-ing them valuable advice.

Norman "Sonny" Kelly-Kinew

Ojibwa

Peter DeCory
Rosebud Sioux

I began dancing late in my life, after I was given my regalia by a relative. He had danced for several years with it, after it was gifted to him by Sam DeCory, also kin to me. Sam DeCory is a Vietnam veteran and belongs to the Red Feather Society for wounds received in battle. Sam made this regalia.

Out of respect for Sam, my father, Kermit DeCory, Sr., and various relatives and friends who served in the armed forces during all past wars, I dedicate my dancing to them. You all have my deepest respect for the sacrifices made for our family and the Lakota Nation.

Percy Casper
Shuswap

In April 1994 I received a Bachelor of Arts degree in anthropology with a minor in linguistics and a certificate in research. I am now finishing a post baccalaureate training in Community Economic Development. In 1995, I received a Native Adult Instructors Diploma. I accomplished this at Simon Fraser University. The reason for mentioning my accomplishment is to encourage young people to pursue their education.

Culture is a common bond that holds our people together, regardless of tribe. Dancing in my regalia also expresses who I am. The drumbeat we dance to is the heartbeat of North America. All nations and tribes have a unique style of dancing; each move has significant meaning. Northern traditional is my style of dress.

Timothy D. Brooks, Sr.
Nez Perce/Colville

I started to dance when I was young. My grandfathers and grandmothers told me to dance like the Eagle Spirit. I like to feel this spirit enter my soul when I dance. It is like no other feeling in the world to me. When I compete in the contest, I sometimes feel this spirit hit me. At that moment, it's like no one else is on the floor but me. I work with native youth and try and teach them that this feeling I get from dancing is better than drinking and drugs. I feel that if we can hold on to our culture, we will have our traditions for a long time to come.

Reginald A. George, Sr.
Nooksac/Nez Perce

There are many reasons why I dance in powwows. There are as many reasons I dance as there are reasons I breathe. If you take my dance, you take away my breath.

I am a Clown Dancer. I will not explain this, you need to learn in your own way. Our coastal relatives wear wooden masks for different reasons. I wear a feather mask because I am also Nez Perce.

People deal with death in many different ways. I dance to heal myself since the passing of my wife and four children. If dance were not so powerful, I would not ask her to help me. You can cut off my legs; I will continue to dance because the song is in my heart. When you return my body to Mother Earth, the coyote will sing my song for me. I will be like the wise salmon and travel home when my life is over.

There are many reasons I travel to powwows, but I will give you one reason I go. Once, I asked a non-Indian, church-going friend why he was raising money to go to the Holy Land. My non-Indian brother told me that in the Holy Land there were spiritual men who had visions that came true. My friend told me there were spiritual men who could actually talk with the animals. I told my friend that in Indian Country there were spiritual men who had visions that came true. I told my friend that in Indian Country there were acts of great healings. I told my friend that in Indian Country there were spiritual men who could actually talk with the animals. I told my friend that Indian Country is Holy Land.

CHAPTER FOUR

NATIVE PRIDE— GIFT OF IDENTITY

BOB RED ELK (LITTLE WARRIOR)

ASSINIBOINE/BLACKFEET/
HUNKPAPA, SANTEE,
YANKTON SIOUX

Being Indian is the discovery of our relationship with self, other cultures, the animal world, and the elements (fire, earth, water, air). These together show us that a concept of God has to include all living things. To others we may appear unique; perhaps they are seeing that individual or group of individuals discovering their place on this earth and in the universe.

DARLYNE SHORTMAN

GROS VENTRE / CHEYENNE

Although I do not dance as a contestant, attending powwows and participating as a women's traditional dancer makes me proud. On the powwow trail I feel the strong spirit of the songs and drums. I am the only dancer in my family. When I dance it is for my children, grandchildren, and all my relatives. At many powwows I have felt the spirit of a song or drum. I pray while dancing, for all my relatives, including those unable to dance because of sickness or being in mourning. When the powwow trail opens, I'm happy to see old friends, meet new ones, and feel the spirit of the drums and songs. I love the excitement of Grand Entry, and, most of all, seeing the beauty of the dancers in regalia. I am proud of my heritage.

ESTHER GEORGE

YAKAMA

I've been dancing since the age of eleven. My son Joseph (see page 8), and I powwow throughout the Northwest.

This past summer, I lost four people in my family and two family friends passed away. In our traditions, we quit dancing for a year when someone dies. It is really hard to go to a powwow and sit on the side to watch. The songs the drummers sing just make you want to dance. My year will come and I will dance again, but it won't be the same as it was. There will be people missing from Grand Entry that we are used to seeing.

Powwow is sacred to me because it keeps me and my son close. In the beginning of summer, we have the calendar marked for the powwow season. I will be back to the powwow circle, but people will be missed.

DERWIN VELARDE
JICARILLA APACHE

One day, my grandmother chuckled as she
recalled that as children we would gather, deco-
rate, and wear sunflowers as regalia and imitate
powwow songs and dances. Although I was too
young to remember, I've always felt the spirit of
the drumbeat. Traditional dancing strengthens my
spirit. Good blessings can come from respecting
our creator, Mother Earth, the heartbeat, and the
circle of life.

GEORGE KICKING WOMAN, NI OKS KAINA

BLACKFEET

(An elder and traditional spiritual leader of the Blackfeet Tribe, George and his wife, Molly, are the keepers of the Long Time Thunder Medicine Pipe. George dances clockwise at the North American Indian Day Celebration each year. He has a beaded buckskin suit with a full headdress. George has given a large portion of his time to maintaining the songs, beliefs, and values of the tribe. He is also an international elder for the keepers of the Medicine Pipes on the Blackfoot Confederacy reserves. He commits his time and energy to honoring all medicine pipes throughout the spring of each year, serving as an advisor to all people desiring to know the ways of his tribe.)

"I was told by the old people when I was young to learn the old ceremonial ways. I feel that through their guidance and the guidance of spirits, my path was set. I feel I was specially selected to learn the songs and the ritual. Some of this has come through visions or dreams. Once when I was on Chief Mountain (our holy mountain), I heard voices of people. I couldn't make out what they were saying, but I know somebody was there. My outfit represents me and my surrounding environment. I dance because it makes me feel good. I want to be remembered, when people see my picture, as a person who helped preserve our culture."

DOUGLAS DAVID,
KWI-A-CEEK

NOOTKA

JERRILYN F. HAMLEY

TURTLE MOUNTAIN CHIPPEWA

Dancing for me is a creative release of emotions. Everything I feel positive about being a Native American is expressed through my dance movement. How I hold myself, my foot movement to the beat of the drum, my braided hair, feathers, buckskin dress and moccasins, all mirror an image of pride in my heritage. Dancing with others of like mind and heart is truly one of the highest forms of spirituality, and that is what dancing is for me.

GERROD MOSES GOUDY, WIN-WY-TIT (GREAT HANDS IN BATTLE)

YAKAMA

My style of dancing is traditional. My outfit was made by my father and me. The bustles are eagle feathers; the other parts are cloth, beaded cloth, ermine skins, buckskin, and various materials. When I dance, I feel pride and the gratitude to our Creator for being who we are, his creation. Although the government attempts to destroy our heritage to make us the same as the dominant societies, our ways have survived. I believe one cannot destroy the Creator's purpose.

KELI SMITH • TSIMSHIAN

(Written by her grandmother, Teresa Bariquit.)
"When I hear my granddaughter reply 'I am Tsimshian' to the question who she is, my heart grows with pride. At last I have lived to see my grandchildren grasp a part of my culture and it is very dear to my heart. All of my life I have tried to gather all of the information of my tribe, so that I can store it away in my memory. Now finally, I am giving my cultural gift to my granddaughters. As I hear my granddaughter speak, I know that I have passed on my pride as a Tsimshian."

MARTY M. PINNECOOSE (EAGLE CHILD)
SOUTHERN UTE / JICARILLA APACHE

The outfit I'm wearing is a fancy dance outfit consisting of two feather bustles. They are made from either turkey feathers or eagle feathers. The hackles (little feathers) that hang from each feather are dyed rooster feathers. I chose the colors and the pattern of my outfit. These are sky colors from my Indian name. The pattern—small diamond shapes— stands for the mountains that surround my people.

Fancy dancing started from the in mid-1950s, when younger men didn't want to dance the slow traditional style. I have been fancy dancing since I was seven years old, and gradually made a name for myself.

(ABOVE) TIMMY GRAY

COWICHAN / NUU-CHAH-NULTH NATIONS AND

(OPPOSITE) JOE "J.T." THORNE, JR.

COWICHAN / NUU-CHAH-NULTH NATIONS

(Timmy Gray is a ten-year-old traditional dancer who has traveled throughout the U. S. and Canada. Joe "J.T." Thorne, Jr., is nine years old and is both a grass and fancy dancer. Both boys live in British Columbia and are members of The Little Raven Dancers; they hoop dance with forty hoops each. They sing and represent the National Aboriginal Veterans Association. All proceeds made by Raven members are donated to charity.)

FLORENTINO "TINY" BARRIL ◆ TLINGIT

I was born in Juneau, Alaska, into an ethnically diverse family. My father emigrated from the Philippines to work in the Alaskan gold, fishing, and timber industry. My mother belonged to the Tlingit Indian Nation, which inhabits the southern and southeastern regions of Alaska. I am proud of my father's heritage and the fact that my name reflects my Filipino roots, but growing up among the Tlingit culture, I was strongly influenced by my mother's side of the family. I now live in Olympia, Washington, and further my tradition as part of a group of fellow Tlingits who don ceremonial dress and perform traditional songs and dances at ceremonies, special events, and public occasions. My dress is culturally rich and impressive. It is made up of furs, skins, and shells, which reflect the Tlingit's fur trading and maritime commerce. One of my headdresses is a hat made of woven red cedar bark with a colorful raven (y'eil) — symbolizing my clan — and a humpback whale (y'aay) painted on it. My other headdress is made of ermine and arctic fox, with a carving of the raven and a human face below. It is called a shakee-at dance headdress.

I feel fortunate to be born to a rich and proud people. When I begin to dress in my regalia, my heart pounds with excitement; I know I will soon dance and sing the songs of my ancestors who have long passed to the spirit world. I dance for my mother, grandmother, and their fathers' people. I will always carry myself with pride and with my head held high, for I know my identity.

WILLIAM R. LANE
LUMMI/MUCKLESHOOT/
METLAKATLA

Before I dance, I talk to each feather and pray with it and thank it for sacrificing its life for me to wear. Each feather has a story to tell. I will always carry and wear feathers with respect and honor. When I go to pow-wows, I celebrate, because I feel in my heart that the people before us did a lot of sacrificing, so this is our time to think of them. When I dance I'm think-ing of the people who came before us. When I dance I have so much pride, joy, and happi-ness that I feel like crying.

WAYLON McCLOUD YALLUP
YAKAMA

VIRGIL T. MATHIAS
KOOTENAI

I am proud to be a full-blooded Kootenai from the Confederated Salish and Kootenai Tribes of Montana's Flathead Nation. The regalia I'm wearing was made by several members of my family, with many parts given to me by friends—porcupine roach (headdress) with owl feathers, eagle head staff, bear claw necklace, bone breastplate, antique bells. My bustle is a powerful display of eagle feathers given to me by my brother. The American flag is placed in the center of the bustle as my expression of pride for my country. I dance to honor my friends and family.

EARL LONEIA (LITTLE BEAR)
SKOKOMISH/SUQUAMISH/ FRASER RIVER/CHILEAN

My dance is the Sacred Spirit Eagle Dance. This dance calls upon Grandfather to forgive us for our mistakes, and to receive thanks for the many blessings he has given us. We ask that he bless all of our sisters and brothers. It has been difficult adapting a coastal dance to the Plains-style Pa Uah manner of contest dancing, but with much prayer and guidance from my elders and friends it is happening really well.

I try to dance in spirit. I dance for the forgiveness and blessings that may come to us. When I enter the arbor for the competition portion, I ask a prayer and offer myself to be used as He will. As I do the Eagle Spirit Dance, I soar over the mountains, trees, lakes, and valleys. I join other eagles, and feel to the core of my soul the power and spirit of my winged cousins, never becoming fatigued or winded.

In my Eagle Spirit Dance, I don't dance to win. I dance for my people, all my people, not just First Nations people, but the Red, Yellow, Black, and White, the medicine wheel colors, and the four directions.

Chapter Five

Family of the Sacred Circle

Bette' Tillequots
Nez Perce/Yakama

The dress that I am wearing belonged to my sister. Her name was Gina. She bought the dress several years ago and began to make the accessories to go with it. She started with moccasins, leggings, cuffs, hair ties, medallions, barrettes, and earrings. All matched the design she chose herself. She had only used her outfit a few times, when she was killed in a snowmobile accident. Our family then put her dress away until we were able to have the memorial ceremony for her.

When our family brought this dress out to be used again, I was the one chosen to wear it in her honor. This is only the second time I have worn this outfit. I am always proud to wear it because I used to watch my sister do the beadwork. She would spend hours at a time beadworking.

Chucky C. Fryberg
Tulalip

I have been dancing since I could walk, and I have a lot of friends on the powwow trail.

I was fancy dancer when this picture was taken. Now I am a traditional dancer.

Chibron (Bron) Tomeo
Salish/Colville/ Gros Ventre/Sioux/ Yakama/Nez Perce

(Bron was born in 1986 and began dancing on his mother's knee. He would move his head, keeping perfect unison with the beat of the drum. Bron is an all-around dancer. He dances traditional, grass, and fancy bustle. His favorite is traditional. Very soon he will be the owner of an eagle bustle. At present, he dances with a hawk feather bustle. He has won numerous championships at pow-wows. There are twenty-six dancers in his large family. The younger ones, from toddlers to teens, are trained by their uncle Rocco Clark.)

Dorothea Romero and Amy Starr Lincoln ◆ Tlingit

Dorothea and her eldest daughter, Amy, are Raven/Beaver from House at the end of Spring Road (Dei-shee-Taan), in Alaska. Dorothea is a self-taught artist, and through her study of her Tlingit heritage she has incorporated Tlingit stories and mythology into her artwork. Recently, Dorothea took two years from her work to attend special training from elders, learning the design and construction of cedar bark hats and basketry. Dorothea honors her ancestry by keeping Tlingit art alive.

Dorothea and Amy have performed their traditional songs and dances at powwows in Montana, California, Oregon, and Washington. Amy's daughters and Dorothea's granddaughters dance the Alaskan dances and do powwow dancing. They believe it helps their self esteem to be part of the cultural exchange by doing their Alaskan dances at powwows. "We know who we are, and have respect for all Nations."

Dawn M. Crōm
Blackfeet Nation

Dancing for me is more than just getting dressed up and moving to the beat of the drum. It's like a state of mind. When I'm dancing, I feel as though nothing else matters. It takes me away to a place where serenity lasts forever. When I'm dancing, it's not only for God, it's for all the people who have inspired me throughout my travels. Most of all, my inspiration came from my parents; my mother's encouragement has taught me to be the best that I can be, and my father's belief in me has helped me to believe in myself and know that I can do anything I set my mind to.

Francis J. Cullooyah,
T-Shel-Shu-Lex
(Stands on The Ground)
Kalispel/Flathead

Here is a prayer: We give thanks, to Creator, for our pride, and the spirit within us. We give thanks, to Creator, for our grandmothers, our mothers, our sisters, our brothers, our nieces, our nephews, our aunts, our uncles, and our little cousins. We give thanks, to Creator, for the many voices of the animal spirits. We give thanks, to Creator, for the teachings, and for the dancing of our elders. We give thanks, to Creator, for the memories of the ones now gone, the ones who smiled and danced beside us. And, thank you Grandfather, for pow-wows, the beating of the drum, as it unites all tribal nations, and revives the heartbeat of all. Grandfather, Creator of all, thank you for my heritage.

Gary Abrahamson ◆ Colville

Jerome P. Tsinnajinnie and LaDonna Starr ◆ Dineh

Jerome: I was told by my Uncle Jim that while my mother was carrying me she participated in many celebrations. Before I started walking, I would just bounce to the drumbeat. My parents took me to many powwows. That's when I started dancing. To feel the beat and dance is a gift given to me before I was born. At one powwow, I did not have an outfit. My grandma and mom tried to get me out of the circle. The traditional dancers were getting ready to contest. I just stood there and watched them. The Arena Director said, "Let him be. He is not in the way." So, they left me to bounce with the elders. After the contest, people came up to me, shook my hand, and gave me money. The gifts helped me to get my traditional outfit. My family helped with my regalia. To this day, I am still blessed with items from all my relatives.

LaDonna: I was very sociable as a child. I started powwow at an early age, but I didn't take to dancing like my older brother. At the age of five, my first outfit was my mom's ribbon dress. My parents always knew where to find me; running and playing with my outfit on with the other kids. I like to attend powwows because I like to meet people and make friends. When I have my jiggle dress on, people come up to me and ask questions about my outfit: who made this, who beaded that, where do you get all those cones? My grandparents tell me, "Powwow is a place where young people can enjoy themselves without getting into trouble or using drugs." They always know where to find us kids—dancing in the circle.

John Cannepotato (People Walking Side-by-Side) ◆ Cree

I started dancing at the age of fourteen. I was inspired as a dancer by my uncle, Joe Saddleback, of Hobbema, Alberta. I left powwow for some years, but the tradition stayed with me. That is why I decided to take part again. I believe this culture and way of life is what keeps our families together: the Great Spirit who guides us has a purpose. In the unity of Indian gatherings, His family are participants in powwow. It is not winning at a powwow, it is the dancing spirit that keeps us, gives us life, gives us strength and love for our families, relatives, and others.

Martin Whelshula,
Yen Chee Chin
Sanpoil Band of the Colville
Confederated Tribes

During my childhood I spent a lot of time traveling with my family to powwows. I quit dancing in my adolescence, but always knew I would dance again. In 1986 I was inspired by the Spokane tribe's powwow to begin dancing again. At first my wife helped me with my outfit, but now I do my own beadwork and feather work. Each year my outfit changes and evolves as it reflects my inner spirit. I love dancing, especially when my children and family are on the dance floor with me. When the drum sounds it connects the spirits of all the dancers. To dance is to celebrate life.

Johnny Lehi, Jr.
San Juan Southern Paiute

I started dancing at a very young age and still enjoy dancing and traveling to different powwows in and out of Arizona. I am from Hidden Springs, Arizona. The colors that I wear represent my tribe and elders who have given me advice. I am fluent in Paiute, Navajo, and English. I would also like to learn other languages as well. I have been raised with traditional values, and respect what I've been taught.

Peter Anthony (Sky Eagle)
Shuswap

I am from the interior plateau of British Columbia, Canada. The traditional dance regalia that I wear derives from the history of my people, but its most important aspect is that it represents my family, past and present. The dance style I do has been developed through many spiritual ceremonies and visions adapted to my natural ability.

Peter Olney, Sr., and Peter Joe Olney, Jr.
Yakama

(Peter Olney, Sr., a seventy-three-year old World War Two Navy veteran, was introduced into the circle of dancing in the 1930s by the Yakama chief Jim Looney. Olney recalls: "In those days, dancing was more spiritual; dancing for prizes or money was unheard of on our reservation. The celebrations were more isolated, with local Indians and a few neighboring tribes attending. Today, native people travel hundreds of miles to visit and compete, to share cultural foods, and exchange tradition. The one thing that has not changed is the belief in the Creator and his laws to guide us to walk in harmony with the universe." Peter Joe, Jr., his wife, Audrey, and their five children are all dancers; they have been international champions in their categories.)

Ron Walsey
Warm Springs

I have been dancing since I was in diapers, and all of my children have been raised the same way. The design of my outfit came to me as a vision in the sweat lodge long ago. My wife, Edith, made the outfit: the yellow shows the sun as the earth comes alive; black represents night as the earth goes back to sleep. The feather hat is Mandan/Hidatsa style. Originally only men who kept order could wear this type of hat. The eagle head on the staff is very old and came from an elder in Pine Ridge.

Rudy R. Shebala
Dineh

Because I grew up among Nez Perce people of Idaho I adopt the Plains style in my dance regalia. My desire is to continue the life of my ancestors. My childhood was filled with tales of Indian heroes. Their actions dictated the lifestyle that I am striving to achieve. I shall not fail. I shall not be the one that does not pass on my ancestor's teachings. I know a few things that will forever dictate who are to be my gods, what are to be my values and morals, and, above all, I know that my thoughts, hopes, dreams, and beliefs are from the point of view of my ancestors.

Ixtlixochitl I. Salinas and Joanna Citlali Salinas ◆ Aztec

We are Aztec, from the town of Tacuba in Mexico City, Mexico. We come from a traditional family well known as dancers, artisans, and merchants. Back home, we go to festivities every weekend, mostly in and around the city. Our tradition is not just about dancing, it's a whole family structure. Thanks to our parents, Juan and Blanca Salinas, our family has been able to keep our traditions and prepare for the future.

We have been traveling in the U.S. for ten years, attending cultural events and visiting schools and universities to teach the true history and beauty of our people. We also attend many powwows and gatherings. We are building bridges through our dances: we express our emotions, honoring deities representing elements of nature and life. Every time we dance it feeds our spirit, making us stronger. We have an important task—to teach, share, and learn.

Sophie Francis George ◆ Yakama

I was born near The Dalles, Oregon, at the ancient Indian fishing grounds of Celilo Falls. I grew up on the reservation and along the Columbia River. I started dancing at an early age. My sister entered as a fancy dancer and I entered as a traditional dancer. That is what we still do today. One of the many reasons that I practice traditional dancing is to give a sense of direction for the little children.

Through watching and learning from traditional elders, children can learn the old ways of their people. An elder is chosen to guide and help us through life. The elders told us that things had to be earned, and that even the things you wear are a part of you. And the way you dance, the steps you do when you dance, can tell a story of where you have traveled or what you have done in your lifetime. We are taught that as you grow, you will meet other Indians and learn of their many ways. Always remember who and where you came from. Don't try to be something you're not. When you are brought into the circle, you bring gifts. I have knowledge of a wide range of traditional art forms of my people, including beadwork, basketry, and traditional dancing and ceremonials.

Acknowledgments

A project of this size could not have been accomplished without the aid of many people. First, many thanks go to my Powwow Partner and wife, Linda, whose original ideas about creating a book have now been realized. She has been with me at every powwow setting, from loading the equipment, posing for the Polaroid test shots, and compiling the tribal data, to driving across the Continental Divide in a late May blizzard. Her positive attitude and absolute attention to detail have taken this body of work from the light table in my office to the hands of interested readers across this land.

Thanks to Robert Morton at Abrams for his insight and ability to instantly visualize this book from the first time he viewed some of the sample images sent to him. It was under his guidance and direction that our idea first took form and the final book was created. Bob McKee of Abrams has done a superior job in setting the photographs on the page and choosing type to complement and enhance the pictures.

A special note of thanks goes to Judy Fireman for her publishing experience, diplomacy, encouragement, patience, and great sense of humor while working with us.

A very particular thanks to Bernie Whitebear (Colville), Executive Director of United Indians of all Tribes, whose continued support over the years has allowed my photography project to prosper. The staff of Iw'asil Youth Program in Seattle have allowed me access to the many powwows they have produced. I thank them. If it had not been for Bob Eaglestaff (Lakota Sioux), principal of the American Indian Heritage High School, I would not have gained access to my first powwow. And, of course, heartfelt thanks to all the many people who have allowed me a moment of their time so that all others may see and learn.

Photographic Notes

Much praise should be given to my camera system: the Mamiya RB67 Pro S with a 127mm lens. Even the rigorous use I give this system in my commercial assignments is overshadowed by the treatment it gets on hot, dusty miles spent along the powwow trail. The reliability of the system under a wide variety of diverse and difficult conditions has been superb. Special thanks are due to Henry Froehlich, president of Mamiya America for his great technical expertise, his appreciation of my work, and his unfailing friendship.

For film, I rely on Fuji Velvia, rated at 50 ISO. It recorded the vibrant colors of the dancers' regalia in ultra-fine detail. The rich, warm colors in these images is testament to Velvia's inherent qualities.

The photographic lighting system I use is a Norman 2000 pack with three heads: the key light is a 30 x 40 vertical softbox; the fill light is a 40-inch umbrella positioned behind and to the left of the camera. A small snoot is also on the left of the camera and is pointed at the painted muslin backdrop to give some separation.